FINDING

FAVOR

WITH GOD:

WHAT'S LOVE GOT TO DO WITH IT?

DR. PAUL CRUZ

FINDING FAVOR WITH GOD:

WHAT'S LOVE GOT TO DO WITH IT?

Copyright © 2020 by Dr. Paul O. Cruz

Love Wins Publishing
www.lovewinspub.com
Redlands, California

Printed in the United States of America

First Printing, August 2020

"What's love got to do, got to do with it,
What's love but a secondhand emotion,
What's love got to do, got to do with it,
Who needs a heart when a heart can be broken."
-Tina Turner, 1984

CONTENTS

From the Author

Marriage is such an amazing institution designed and established by our Creator. As far as I am concerned it is the institution that lays the foundation upon which family is built. Marriage is the womb from which the folkways, mores and conventions of social behaviors are born. More than 90 percent of Americans will marry at some point in their lives.

Within the environment of marriage, new generations are formed, nurtured, and introduced into our social structures. By this I do not imply that those generations born out of wedlock are not viable, valuable, and productive, it is just the focus of my writing is direct toward the marital covenant.

The idea of two complete strangers joining themselves together, working to establish a oneness that transcends any similar relationships, in my opinion, is divine.

My marriage to Colette is like other marriages in its generic template. However, it is ultimately unique and different in other ways because we are ultimately unique and different from our peers in marriage.

My intent is not to address the uniqueness of our marriage, as opposed to others, but to examine the broad aspects that we share experientially with all married couples and those involved in the dating relationship.

There are common roadblocks and pitfalls that mark the path to every courtship and marriage that I wanted to be exposed and examined through the lens of my 65 years of life and 34 years of marriage.

This book is my perspective on marriage, constructed using the skills and tools acquired and purchased with personal and academic currency. It is not my intent to project this book as the official canon on marriage, but simply a perspective of experience.

My marriage to and relationship with Colette is a journey fraught with new life lessons, narrative changes, paradigm shifts, periods of tremendous successes and to a lesser degree monumental failure. Nevertheless, it is a journey that is still unfolding, and I am excited about what lies ahead especially because I get to take that journey with my best friend.

Marriage is such an interesting spiritual and social dynamic because no matter how much you plan or how keen your sense of observation is, you will always be at the mercy of the mystery and unexplored depths of your spouse.

The Apostle Paul writes in Ephesians 5:31-32, "For this reason a man will leave his father and mother and be united to his wife, and the two will become one flesh. This mystery is profound, but I am speaking about Christ and the church. So, why did I decide to write this book? It is a mystery to me!

-Dr. Paul O. Cruz

A Word from His Wife

It is not that people plan to fail, but as Benjamin Franklin stated, "If you fail to plan, you are planning to fail!" The author of this book wants you to win and to win at one of the most important endeavors of your life - your marriage. I know you think that you have found heaven in the arms of your mate, but trust me, sometimes it will feel like you have found hell; it will feel like you are in a war.

You will think that your spouse is the enemy - they are not. You are going to need to know who the real enemy is. You are going to need weapons to fight that enemy. The author has given you the weapons you need to win.

These weapons we have acquired and the lessons we learned have been hard earned. You see, I have been married to Dr. Cruz for almost 35 years and we wave our victor's flag proudly.

Plan to take your time as you go through this book. Plan to discuss what you read with your spouse. Plan to be willing to change. Plan to let God's Word settle issues. Plan to win.

To God be the Glory.

Colette Joslin Toomer Cruz

Executive Pastor
Love and Faith Christian Center

CHAPTER 1

WHAT'S LOVE GOT TO DO WITH IT?

What's love got to do with it? It may seem oddly strange to begin a Christian book about marriage and the marriage relationship with words from a popular secular song, especially one that really does not promote marriage but instead relegates one of marriage's most important tenants to the level of mere animal attraction. Yet, it's important to revisit the song's popularity because intertwined in its melodic beats, hard pounding bass lines, and popular lyrics is a resounding message which has stealthily taken root in the hearts and minds of the generations who supported the song's theme by so innocently regurgitating its lyrics over and over and over again.

The lyrics became a theme song for a generation of people, saints, and sinners alike. Yet, the Bible clearly warns about the power of words, warning that by them we are condemned or justified (Matthew 12:36-37). Please, do not misunderstand my reason for spotlighting this particular song; I am in no way trying to infer that this one popular song is the reason for the ills of the world or the seemingly impotent nature of relationships in this present day and time. This song for all intents and purposes identifies and highlights the matrimonial attitudes which pervade our contemporary social persona.

Ok, ok, here is just a sample of the song's lyrics. See if you remember: "You must understand though the touch of your hand makes my pulse react, it's only the thrill of boy meeting girl, opposites attract. It's physical, only logical, you must try to ignore that it means more than that …what's love got to do with it, what's love but a secondhand emotion…." *It is physical, only logical. I like you, you like me, or at least we think we do. Anyway, let us not sweat the small stuff. We have a physical attraction, so it is only logical that we hook up. My place or yours?* What else is there? Indeed, what else is there, besides, what's love got to do with it?

How apropos considering statistics show the divorce rate in this country has reached critical mass and the nuclear family has all but disappeared from view with the exception of the few celluloid reminders that can only be found on the reruns of black and white TV shows on the TVLand channel. What happened to the days when a young man and a young woman daydreamed of the time when they would marry the person of their dreams, buy a house, and raise a family? The time when a young woman would talk with her mother and even her grandmother about how it was when they were planning their weddings. The time when young women had hope chests and the young men had hope.

Let us not get this thing twisted. Even though it was not widely spoken of, young men, too, dreamed of their wedding day, and not just for the obvious reasons. (Come on; let us clean it up, fellas. You see, it is that kind of thinking that is rampant in this sex-crazed society.) Young men in the privacy of their innermost hearts, where pride and gender pressure have no access, whimsically imagined providing a good life for the girl of their dreams. They imagined having the opportunity to raise their children in a safe and happy environment, teaching their sons to play ball and giving them tips on how to win a girl's heart, while teaching their daughter how to avoid getting their heart broken. I heard somewhere (I do not remember where, maybe in a song) those were the "days of yea and nay."

Perhaps at this point you are saying those days are gone and my naiveté is showing. If you knew my history you would know it has nothing to do with being naïve and everything to do with my strong belief and faith that God has designed a system for us to carry out His plan of family. If we would yield to His Word, we could find our way back to the place of obedience and innocence, oh, not the innocence of ignorance but the innocence of believing and trusting in the guiding hand of God.

I know in our sophisticated and technologically evolved world (you see as a Christian I believe in evolution, at least where technology is the issue) that we will never see the days of Ozzie and Harriet or Leave it to Beaver again, at least not from the perspective of life style. I have no problem with that. I mean, no one should be expected to live without satellite TV, streaming, cell phones or microwaves. I mean come on, but what is there to prevent us from returning to that time of moral respectability?

Now before all the pseudo-liberals start getting all up in a tizzy and start Christian-bashing, I'm talking about a time when moral respectability meant, at the least, if you weren't being moral you had enough respect for yourself, those you engaged with, and your neighbors to keep it to yourself. I believe in the God of the Bible, and I believe that the Bible is the inerrant Word of God. I believe that holy men of old spoke as the Holy Spirit gave them utterance. I am not going to argue my beliefs; I don't have to. You see, this is my book and you do not have to continue to read it or keep it; however, if you do, I am confident your life will be improved. I mention my belief and faith in God because I want to establish the foundation and platform that gives rise to the forthcoming thoughts, ideas, and feelings.

CHAPTER 2

SIMPLE ANSWER

I have no interest in being politically correct and I have no interest in offending (at least not
premeditatedly); however, if my ideals and beliefs
as outlined in this book are contrary to what you
believe or what is popularly accepted then let the
chips fall where they may. I have one agenda for
writing this book and that is to see the will of God
done in the lives of all who are sensitive enough to
follow the leading of the Holy Spirit in acquiring
this writing. I specifically want to focus on the institution of marriage, not from the perspective of
statistics and polls but from experience, revelation,
and biblical truth.

I will not spend a lot of time examining or
rebuffing the treacherous attack that Satan has
mounted against God's most sacred institution;
there is enough minutia out there on the subject to
keep you distracted till Christ returns. There are
volumes of information about how badly off marriages are in this country today. Therefore, there is

no need for me to exacerbate the subject by filling these pages with more statistics. Suffice it to say the statistics do not paint a rosy future of marriage in the country.

It does not take much effort to identify what is wrong with marriage these days or to indict the Godly institution of marriage as an outdated and archaic failure. However, what does require tremendous vigor, energy, and steadfastness of spirit is the revival of biblically-based moral living, which will be instrumental in the efforts to de-program this society that has brainwashed and mesmerized itself through its own lust and self-degrading apathy toward God, His Word and His plan of holiness. There is also the critical need to promote and encourage godliness and Christian morality in the male-female relationship. This is necessary to see the institution of marriage recover from its malignant condition and reestablish itself as the ultimate pinnacle of God's expression of purpose for men and women.

All efforts must be directed towards identifying and addressing every morally acceptable avenue of repair and restoration. There needs to be more volumes written on how to prepare for marriage, as well as how to repair marriages, including advice which addresses the spiritual and the pragmatic. Much of what will be discussed in this book will not be new information and that is ok because I read somewhere (I don't know where, maybe it was in Sports Illustrated), that "faith cometh by hearing, and hearing by the Word of God" (Romans 10:17 NKJV).

I believe there is a simple answer to this nation's marital problem, that answer being our return to obedience to the Word of God. How much simpler can it be? Now that I have solved the problem, I guess I should just end the book. I would that it would be that simple. Can you believe that people use to actually speak that way, "I would that it would be so simple"?

Although what I wrote would solve the problem, I cannot just stop there because most of you do not believe or will not believe that it is just that simple. Plus, it would not be fair to make you miss all the stories that I have to tell. Besides, I think that the relationship/marriage information market should be flooded with volumes and volumes of books and magazines, as well as radio and television commercials on preparing for and maintaining a healthy marriage. Why not, it's what being done in the reverse. Just peruse the local newsstand (Are there such things as newsstands anymore?) and see the literature that finds its way there. Many espouse the ideas of independent living (you don't need a husband or wife), shacking, same-sex relationships, and the like. The television airwaves are inundated with shows that promote infidelity, promiscuity, homosexuality, lesbianism, drug and alcohol abuse, and even subtle child pornography.

We are bombarded with these visual and auditory images day in and day out, the insidious master plan intent on desensitizing our moral nerve and causing the sinew of our character to atrophy. All the while, in direct contrast, television shows that have a format to promote the wholesome family, purity and integrity of character, and God are quickly eased out of the primetime slots and ultimately out of our minds. As I take my shot at the marriage subject, I would like to center my focus on one particular passage of scripture, not an unfamiliar one but one that does make a particular point that I have not heard discussed at any length, at least not in my restricted circle of influence - Proverbs 18:22.

Proverbs 18:22, tells us, "He who finds a wife finds a good thing, and obtains favor from the Lord." What favor? As a Christian man aren't I already in the favor of the Lord? Yet, somehow, this portion of scripture seems to imply that the man who negotiates his way through whatever obstacle course life lays out before him and manages to find for himself a covenant wife, somehow positions himself for Godly favor previously not accessible to him. Now that's a spicy meatball!

What an interesting verse of scripture on many levels. The verse in and of itself is not a complex one. On the surface, it appears to be a quite simple statement from the writer: for a man to get married is a good thing, which in turn places him in a good light with God. In my simple existence and limited experience in the service of the Lord, I have come to understand that it is the simple and seemingly passive revelations from God that had the most profound and lasting effect on the individuals who can capture their essence.

I have been married 33 years at the time of this writing; this is my first (and hopefully my only) marriage. I was fortunate enough to marry my best friend. My wife and I had never been intimate in any sexual way prior to our wedding night (not for a lack of trying on my part). As a matter of fact, we had never been on a date in the romantic sense. We will talk more about that later.

There are some basic and simple truths that can be gleaned from the holy words found in Proverbs 18:22. The first being: "He who finds a wife…." I know that what I am about to say will stir up a hornet's nest, but please refer to my disclaimer about not caring about political correctness. That being said, the implication is that the marriage relationship as designed by God - God being the sovereign, righteous, holy, and immutable Creator of all things - was designed to be expressed between a man and a woman.

There is also the explicit inference that the relationship between a man and a woman is to be a monogamous one, monogamy meaning one man or one woman sharing his or her life with one woman or one man. There is no indication that the man should have "girl friends" or "friend girls"; neither should the woman have "boyfriends" or "friend boys." Obviously, there can be exceptions to almost any point in a discussion if your intentions are to be contrary for the sake of being contrary. I am simply pointing out that marriage is difficult enough without the added stress of external emotional influences.

The idea that a man or a woman can successfully integrate their previous plutonic, opposite-sex relationships into their marriage relationship is at best a veiled attempt to hold onto some aspect of their former life and at worst a safety net in case of failure. These types of prior relationships become especially dangerous in times of marital difficulties and emotional distress, which all married couples experience because of two strangers trying to meld into one being. Where is Spock (the Vulcan, not the doctor) when you need him? This melding thing is more than a notion.

When a marriage relationship is going through its metamorphosis, there is absolutely no room for external influences from old male and female friends, especially single ones. Oh, by the way, the marital metamorphosis continues for the duration of the marriage until death does part one from the other. In other words, there is never a time when you should be so emotionally tied to someone of the opposite sex or, for that fact, even the same sex (i.e. "homeboys" or "homegirls"; if you live in the 'burbs then it's "buds" and "girl-friends") to where they present an avenue of escape from your spouse, even if that avenue of escape is only a mental one.

I know that this is not a popular ideology, but if you want to maintain your current social standing then you should not get married. In other words, if you want to keep your old boyfriends or girlfriends as confidants then you should not get married. As previously mentioned, I have been married for 33 years and I can honestly say I don't have any male or female best friends. Of course, there are people with whom I share time and conversations and would even consider some to be friends. Some I would even say I love, but none of them are such that in a time of marital difficulty I would consider as a means of escape or a place of sanctuary from my marriage covenant.

My wife is my best friend. I don't have bowling buddies, football buddies, or any other type of buddies in the sense that we share some intimacy on any level that would exclude my wife's presence or knowledge. When I want to hang out, I hang out with my wife. If she's not available, then nine times out of ten I don't hang out. I also do not have female friends to whom I go for advice on what my wife is thinking or feeling or to share my feelings or thoughts about my wife or our relationship. Do I talk about life issues with those in my circle of influence? Of course, but most of the time it's venting and not counsel seeking.

I do, however, have a pastor from whom me and my wife seek advice, and there are one or two seasoned, married Christian couples who have been instrumental in helping us to secure the sanctity of our marriage. I purposely identified the couples as "married," which may or may not seem redundant depending on your perspective. Unfortunately, even in the Christian community, there are men and women sharing their lives as a couple, attempting to procure the fruits and rewards of marriage all the while perpetuating the false narrative that they can and do possess everything that marriage provides without the seal of the marriage vows. Therefore, it is important that the meaning of a "couple" for the intent of this writing be clearly defined as "married folk."

CHAPTER 3

THE SEARCH BEGINS

I have had close female friends whom I have known for many years, some since high school. You do the math. For the math impaired, I am 65 years old, I have been married for 33 years, and I have some close female friends that I have known since high school, which means that I knew them before my wife. But I do not seek them out nor share with them the life that I share with my wife.

I practice this because I do not want any woman (or man for that fact) to know me on a personal level equal to my wife or as a best friend. My wife is my best friend. Intimacy on the level that I am speaking of is, I believe, reserved for the marriage covenant.

Are there marriages out there that are healthy and secure where the husband and wife have friends of the opposite sex (or same sex) with whom they share their thoughts and feelings and from whom they seek and receive advice? I am sure that there are many. I am by no means utterly dismissing the idea that some marriages can survive like that, but I am cautiously confident that they are the exceptions rather than the rule.

As I reflect over the years of my life, I can clearly identify those women with whom I have shared remarkably close personal relationships. I note, not all a sexual nature. The few that are most prominent in my mind's eye and that bring an instant smile to my face were the ones with whom our relationships were based on mutual respect and intellectual compatibility.

No, these women were not old maids, sexually repressed, or unattractive, whatever that means. I loved and still love them in a special way, but there is a covenant that I share with my wife that disqualifies their inclusion. Oh yeah, by the way, they are also married, successfully, and do not seek me out for advice on their marriages either.

"He who finds a wife...." With all the women in the world of different heights, weight, color, and culture, why would a man have to "find" a wife. Why not just pick one? Why does the Holy Spirit phrase it that way? What is there to *finding* a wife and not picking one?

The word *finds* functions as a verb. Its etymology is Middle English, from Old English *findanas* (akin to Old High German findan- meaning "to find"). I put this information in here just so I could sound like some kind of well-read intellectual. With that thought in mind, who really knows what "Middle English" is? Is it like Hobbit language from Middle Earth? And what the heck is etymology and what does it have to do with marriage? I digress.

Find as defined by the Merriam-Webster Collegiate dictionary means: "*to come upon often accidentally; to come upon by searching or effort; to discover by study or experiment.*" It seems to me that by virtue of the definition of the word *find*, the man who desires to marry has a journey that he must embark upon. This journey, as far as I can tell, has no discernable start date. For all we know it may begin at birth or puberty or at some indiscernible point along the spectrum of life that is not meant to be pinpointed. We can say, with all certainty, that if the man is to be married he must at some point be awakened to the realization that he is indeed on a journey that is meant to conclude with him being joined in covenant with his wife, thereby granting him some special divine favor that cannot be obtained in any other manner.

I find it quite interesting that the word *find* is defined at least in one instance as "to come upon often accidentally." It seems at least in my mind that if we were able to poll all the men who are married and have remained married, more often than not we would find men who did not marry who they imagined they would. What I mean is, the woman of their original mental design in most instances is not the woman who they now love and cherish.

Now this is not an indictment against any relationships but more a substantiation of the definition of the word *find*. I know that I did not marry the type of woman that I had imagined in my mind. I stumbled upon her by accident, "divine accident," if you get my drift. My wife was not the type of woman that I had dated or sought out to date, at least not in terms of wanting a relationship. I use the word "relationship" loosely here because its meaning for me now is quite different than when I was dating. However, as an unsaved man, if the opportunity had presented itself, I would have dated her for immoral reasons, not as a candidate for marriage. I had already formed an image in my mind and psyche as to the type of woman I thought I wanted to marry, if I were to marry at all.

The word *find* is also defined as "to discover by study or experiment." I submit to you that by no stretch of the imagination is this definition a license to explore the pleasures of womanhood through physical study or experimentation. In other words, as a man goes on his journey in search of his wife, he will obviously encounter many women, some who will catch his fancy and others who will not. For those that do as well as those who do not, he does not have biblical permission to sample her wares in an effort to determine if she is the "one."

Ok, so now you gonna act stupid. You know exactly what I mean by "sampling her wares" – no sex before marriage! If you have the urge to sample something, then test drive a car or do some wine or cheese tasting. Go to See's Candy; they will give you some samples. "Take the red pill, Neo."

I believe that one of the key issues that relationships face today is that there is no sincere study and discovery time involved. I read somewhere (I don't exactly remember where), perhaps it was 1 Peter 3:7a (NLT), the words, "Husbands, in the same way you must give honor to your wives. Treat your wife with understanding as you live together." *Treat your wife with understanding.* It is obvious that there is level of understanding that a man must obtain in order to have a peaceful and successful co-existence with his wife.

There are two critical identifying factors that support marriage biblically, "husbands dwell/live with your wives...." Ephesians 5:25. This clearly dismisses the idea of shacking. If you are going to dwell/live in the framework of marriage, then you should be husband and wife. It is my modest position that the introduction to the understanding process begins with the searching process. As a man interacts with the woman in his life, he begins his understanding process and that process terminates when death does him and his wife part.

It is my contention that if a man desires to understand a woman he must learn from women. I'm not encouraging men to become effeminate, but I am encouraging men to study and observe and internalize information that women give. I am not talking about getting to know your softer side or the hidden woman within yourself. If you are dealing with those types of issues, get counseling. You are heading down a slippery slope.

I am talking about the fact that I believe women are constantly and continuously exposing themselves to men and are quietly shouting, "Here I am, understand me!" I do not believe that God would instruct men to dwell with their wives according to understanding if they were not open to being understood themselves.

Let me give you one example from my life. As I said before, my wife and I are best friends. We were best friends five years before we got married, we never dated, nor were we intimate until our wedding night. We were road dogs. We traveled together and hung out, drank beer, and watched football together. We shared our singleness with one another. I married my best friend so you would think that with this type of history our marriage would not have the problems that other marriages have.

Here is my point: with all that history behind us, in or around the sixth or seventh year of our marriage, a marriage that I thought was going pretty well, my wife asked for a divorce. Let me interject here that my wife, Colette, and I never use foul language and have never used it towards one another. We do not yell or scream at one another and since the first year of our marriage there have been no physical altercations in our relationship (There was one incident only, it was my fault, I might discuss it later).

So, you can imagine my shock when she started talking about divorce. As we talked, she kept saying that I was not giving her what she needed and I kept on saying and thinking, "What more can you want? You have your own money, your own car, house, etc. I do not follow you around to see where you are; you come and go as you please, without being hounded. What more could you want?"

I know that the women reading this noticed immediately what was wrong with our relation-ship, and some of you men who are wiser than you look picked up on it as well. However, it took me a while with many tears and serious marital coun-seling to understand the problem. If you did not catch it, I will explain. My wife was saying to me, "You are not giving me what I need," and I was hearing, "You are not giving me what I want." Big, big, big difference.

As a man, I equated houses, cars, money, and social freedom with her "need," because for me all those things met my needs. But for my wife, they left her longing. What I found out is what she needed was to know that of all that was seemingly important in life (houses, cars, money, and posses-sions) she was most valuable to me. To fill her void in our relationship she needed to feel and know that I would protect and value her more than anyone or anything.

You see, fellas, she could buy for herself all the things that I had given her, and quiet as it is kept, she did buy most of what she had or at least shared in the purchases. The thing that made it all valuable to her was not something that she or I could purchase with money. Now here is the sad part: for seven years she was quietly shouting at me, "Here I am, see me!"

CHAPTER 4

STUDY HALL

Now, when God says, "he who finds…." There is much more involved than just hooking up. God is talking about study and experimentation.

In 2 Timothy 2:15 the Word tells us to "study to show ourselves approved unto God…." It is always assumed that He is speaking only of the scripture, but I submit for your consideration that His instruction extends even into our relationships.

Initially, men need to study themselves. Men need to learn about who they really are spiritually and emotionally. Men need to examine how God has designed and engineered them and how to fit into His divine scheme without disrupting its continuity. What are your thresholds of resistance, acceptance, assurance, confidence, and obedience? Men need to understand that they are hunters by nature (we will talk more about that later) and because of that nature there are complexities which must be resolved so that they can be more easily incorporated into familial life.

One complexity that must be resolved is the difference between manhood and maleness. Every man is a male, but not every male is a man. The understanding of the difference must be viewed from two separate but mutually inclusive perspectives, the first being God's and the second being that of a woman.

There is a standard that has been established in the Word of God by which a man is to carry himself. I could spend the next ten pages quoting scripture to support my statement but suffice it to say that two words characterize God's criteria for Christian manhood - character and integrity. Now, oddly enough, if you ask women about what they want in a man you would more than likely hear these same two words or some variation of them.

Headship is another of those complexities that must be resolved in the heart of men. Men must understand that headship does not automatically translate to mean lordship. Headship and lordship demand prerequisites of fidelity, commitment, accountability, stewardship, worship, submission, repentance, and obedience - these being the fundamental building blocks for a strong foundation. The list is inexhaustible as there are other responsibilities which are supplemental. There is much a male must learn about manhood as he endeavors to pursue God's plan and purpose for him where women and wives are concerned.

Additionally, another complexity in the pursuit of manhood is what I call the "helpmeet syndrome." God calls the woman man's helpmeet. She is provided to man to help him. I believe that she was made from man, and for man, for the purpose of procreation, and I believe that procreation, as important as it is, is only a small aspect of her responsibility.

You see the act of initiating procreation only lasts a couple of hours. *Yeah, right*. Ok, an hour. *Men are such liars*, alright. A couple of minutes and afterward comes the responsibility. My point is this: I believe that she is given to man to teach him the intricacies of manhood that would otherwise escape him.

I believe that she is called a helpmeet because she has within her essence all that is required to help a man meet his godly potential. She can reflect to him his characteristics and attitudes, positive and negative. These are projections of himself that he cannot see or refuses to acknowledge, characteristics and attitudes that in many cases his friends and family will only tolerate rather than address.

The woman who is his true helpmeet has within her the balm that can soothe his injuries and the courage that can fuel his passion. The Bible says the she is the glory of the man. Unfortunately, in the "helpmeet syndrome" many men, Christian men, do not employ the gifts inherent in the wife because he has been socialized to believe that she is the weaker vessel, when in truth the scripture speaks to his treatment of her "as" the weaker vessel and in no wise infers or implies that she is actually weaker. However, because of misinterpretation, misunderstanding, and misogynistic socialization many men view her for the most part as being unqualified to significantly impart into his life on any cogent level, much to his own detriment. She is perceived as being flawed by sensitivity and emotion which cloud and control her ability to be rational in times of stress. Isn't that right Jochebed, Deborah, Ruth, Naomi, Esther, and yes, even Rahab?

I know, because even after 33 years of marriage I still suffer from the residual effects of the "helpmeet syndrome." Let me explain the syndrome this way…my wife says that if she wants me to hear and accept her important input, she will tell it to a man and let him tell me because if I hear it from a man then it must be true, important, or correct. What can I say, I have been married 33 years, but I have been male 65 years. The truth is such a bitter pill to swallow.

My brothers, that is the "helpmeet syndrome." If a woman says it, I'm not sure, but if it comes from a man then it's o.k. As part of our self-examination, we must learn to hear and accept the advice and instruction from our wives, sisters, mothers, aunts. It is odd but for some reason I think God talks to them, too. The nerve!

Men need to examine and study themselves, and even more importantly they need to study the women that they are exposed to. You will not gain understanding about your wife only from your wife. You see, by the time you meet and marry her you should have already gained some much needed and useful information about women from other women. I know that you are thinking. All women are not the same. I would have to agree with you, just like all men are not the same. But just like men have certain innate characteristics and needs, so do women. We gain understanding of our wives as we learn to understand women in general. I hear many men say that there is no way to understand women and I must admit that the challenge is a daunting one; however, if the Lord has instructed us to understand them, then it must be possible on some level.

Let me take this time to drop a little salt into the game. Women, please understand that men are hunters by nature. You call us dogs but that is not entirely accurate. Men are hunters and we enjoy the hunt. Men actually do enjoy the process of courting. With all its twists and turns and with all its heartaches and pains, it is still the hunt that we most enjoy. I mention this because I am often a curious observer to what has become the pitiful spectacle of women hunting men. Women who are ignorantly caught up in the subtly of the delusion that somehow the gulf between men and women has been effectively eradicated, allowing that the natural propensities that separate the sexes are no longer applicable.

We live in the age of heterosexuals, homo-sexuals, bisexuals, asexuals, polysexuals, pansex-uals, transsexualism, gender identifiers, and metrosexuals. I'm not too sure about that last one. Are these people who prefer sex on the Metrorail? Ok, I'm being facetious. Now this may sound a lit-tle Neanderthal, but because women wear tailored suits to work, deserve to earn equal pay with men, get their hair cut at barbershops, sit atop Fortune 500 companies, and smoke cigars, does not abate what is naturally instinctive to men, that being the desire to hunt and not be hunted.

Don't get it twisted. If you insist on hunting a man, he will play the role of prey and will seem-ingly submit and subject himself to your advances as long as there is a benefit for him. He will accept your gifts, your money, the use of your vehicles, your homes, and your intimacy as long as it does not interfere with or hinder his ability to hunt until he is caught (I will explain this statement in a few moments). Bow wow wow, yippee yo yippee yeah.

I see it time and time again where a woman has pursued a man as if she were a man pursuing a woman only to find that in the end, she has ex-hausted herself financially and emotionally and is left holding her heart in her hand. If she is fortu-nate, that is all that she is left having to hold, if you catch my drift. You see, for all the bravado that men spew about the women who pursue them, they are keenly more interested and enamored with the ones that shun and resist them. You know the old adage, "We always want what we can't have."

Here is where I explain my earlier statement that men will allow a woman to pursue him as long as it doesn't hinder his ability to hunt until he is caught. My sixth-grade teacher imparted this nugget of wisdom to a group of us boys during P.E. class where he caught us ogling some of the girls during their P.E. workout. To this day his words still resonate in my mind: "Boys, know this, that a man chases a woman until she catches him." Now at the age of ten or eleven, we kinda laughed it off as the nonsensical ramblings of an old guy; but as time went by and my urge to hunt grew stronger, my experiences began to reveal to me the accuracy of his statement.

The women that pursued me I used mostly as a tool to massage my ego and repair my self-esteem which had been damaged or broken by those women whom I had pursued but who had rejected my advances. I do not mean to infer that I did not care or feel for those women. I am not without compassion, but the truth be told, as a man it was against my nature to be domesticated by a captor whom I did not hunt.

I made this detour because it is fundamentally important to recognize that despite all our technological and social advancements, the baser instincts of men and women remain solidly intact.

When God wrote "he who finds a wife…," that is exactly what He meant. Ladies, it is critically important that you recognize that you are the prize and you determine who finds you and you determine if you want to catch him. Trust me; be patient. You are being hunted.

CHAPTER 5

EXAMINATION

Proverbs 18:22 speaks about finding a "wife." We have examined at least to some extent the idea of "finding" but obviously the object of the finding is the "wife." Therefore, it stands to reason that we should examine the wife. Who is she, what is her role, and what is it about her that so inspires God that when a man finds her, He affords him some measure of special favor?

I will take just a moment for clarification, and I apologize for not being more careful in my description when referring to "a wife." Let's be absolutely clear that I am speaking of a godly, spirit-filled woman, a woman who loves God more than any man that she might catch. If you are curious as to what that woman/wife looks like, then you might peruse Proverbs 31 for some biblical insight.

For as long as I can remember the focus and emphasis has been placed solely on the man within the framework of the proverb and the promised benefits that are his to reap as a result of seeking out and finding a wife. The danger of such myopic thinking is to presume that the means, not the end, is the incentive which causes the hand of God to move on man's behalf. Here we must be careful not to become presumptuous in our autopsy of this proverb to the extent that our findings reflect what is obvious and generic, thereby, pointing us to a false and misleading conclusion. True enough there is the overt pronouncement that when a man finds a wife, it is a good thing and that God will be well pleased with him. However, it would be disingenuous and delinquent for any student of scripture, regardless of their level of scholarship, to assume that there are no more intricacies to the pronouncement than what is written on the surface.

At first glance the obvious implication seems to be that the "man" in this proverb is who God seeks to reward. It is exactly this kind of cursory examination that must be avoided for with it comes the subtle and unconscious tendency of men to diminish and sometimes even dismiss the relevance and importance of the role women play in his development from male, to man, to husband, even as she goes through her own metamorphosis of being prepared to be found as a wife. My assertion is that in the minds of too many men (and, sadly, too many women as well) who read this verse of scripture to believe that the woman's role has been consigned by God himself to be the equivalence of pets in a pet store waiting for some child with his parents or some lonely individual seeking companionship wandering in and choosing them from among the many pets available.

The impression is that the woman merely has to be still and her knight in shining armor will appear and whisk her away to Camelot. I know that this is an oversimplification, but I make it for emphasis. The role of the woman, especially the Christian woman, is one of significance and is critical to the well-being, maturation, and the definitive development from maleness to manhood to husband-hood and by virtue of its importance is worthy of critical analysis.

Is "husband-hood" even a word? I guess it is now. I mean, really, who determines what a word is or what a word isn't? Is there some secret word agency tucked away in the basement of a clandestine government black ops site where seedy characters monitor the airwaves and literary sites for people using non-approved words? Conspiracy theorists hit me back.

Alright, I'm back. At the risk of sounding condescending, I want to make it clear that I am unabridged in my belief that it takes a man to raise a man, but it is also quite clear to me that the influence a woman has on a male's development is also a substantial one. No matter how much influence and affection a father may have with his son or male charge, it never fails when that son or male charge dreams of his future or when he reaches some pinnacle of success and the question is asked of him, "What are you going to do now?" Or when he looks into the camera after some successful event to invariably say, "I'm going to buy my mom a new house," or he's going to look into that camera and with the biggest grin, say, "Hi Mom!" that you see her influence on him is greater and more intimate than we may want to admit.

Who is she, this woman, this wife? The Bible says she is a helpmeet (helpmate), made because, "…there was not found a helper suitable (corresponding to) for him," the *him* being the man [Adam] (Genesis 2:20b NAS). She was created to be a help to man, so often the interpretation of her formation is restricted to childbearing, homemaking, and as a love interest for the man (I use the word "love" loosely here).

I submit to you that God's plan for her in his scheme of creation was not to limit her to being the obedient, robotic, ever present, and ever-available pleasure toy for some self-centered, egomaniacal, sex-crazed, infantile male. Hey, ease up on a brother! I hear you. Instead, she was made so that the man might grow and evolve spiritually, emotionally, and responsibly. Her ability to bear children is only one aspect of her viability and will be less focused on in this writing. She has equality with man, naturally, by virtue of her creation. I know that this flies in the face of many traditionalists within the Christian ranks, but I do not care.

I believe that in Genesis 2:23 when the man ("ish") mouthed the words "this is now bone of my bones, and flesh of my flesh; she shall be called woman ("ishshah"), because she was taken out of man," he was fully aware of her equality with him and her importance to him. If you take note and look closely, you will find within that very procla-mation of the man, an initial and critically im-portant transposition and transformation that oc-curs with regards to his understanding of his rela-tionship to the woman. When the man speaks, he begins by identifying this new creature as "this" but by the time he completes his classification of her, she has made the transformation and transpo-sition from being without category or position to being "woman," the "mother of all living," and the most intimate of all God's creatures to the man. She is "now bone of my bone and flesh of my flesh…." There can be no closer relationship.

The man states that, "she is now…," not that at some point in the future, after I have trained her and put her through her paces, she will become my organic, spiritual, and social equal. Right now. Physiologically a woman and a man are equal, with the exception of the obvious anatomical dif-ferences. However, there is nothing natural in the creation story that speaks about the man being su-perior to the woman to the point she must be sub-servient to him in all aspects of life.

There is, nevertheless, a spiritual hierarchy ordained by the Supreme Creator and Architect, God, who establishes a divine flow chart of re-sponsibility. But let's not deceive ourselves into thinking that because God has established a particular order that the order itself somehow determines an individual's worth based on their position in that order or God's assignment of their gender. Yes, God's assignment of gender! Not gonna fight with you on this. It has often been proved that the ones at the head are not necessarily the ones with the expertise or the know-how; rather, they are adept at recognizing and utilizing the skills of those subordinate to them for the greater good.

As the man goes along on his journey in search of a wife, the woman, too, is on a journey herself. She is learning about what it means to be a woman, what it means to be a godly woman, what it means to be in relationship with Christ and relationship with man. On her journey, she is establishing her protocols, her guidelines, her parameters. She is not sitting at home with her bags packed waiting to be rescued. Quite the contrary, she is out testing her metal in circumstances and situations that will hone her skills, sharpening her insight, building her endurance, and testing her emotional balance, all of which will prepare her to seize upon her rightful place in the heart and home of her husband.

She must see herself and prepare herself as a teacher of men, not a usurper or replacement for them. She will teach her husband what he cannot learn from other men, how she is to be integrated into the very fabric of his life. As his wife, she will teach him that when he trusts her, she will lead him to parts of himself that he has known but not understood because the understanding was hidden in her when she was shaped in secret, understanding that can only be released when she is touched by the spiritually biometric heart print of her divinely ordained mate.

His wife will see for her husband when his eyes have exhausted their ability to see, not for a lack of looking but for his inability to see because he is a man. So many important issues that affect him are invisible to him because they can only be perceived through the experience of his wife. Without her he would stumble past them or into them and, in either case, ruin them.

CHAPTER 6

THEM, NOT JUST HIM

Should a woman be looking for her husband? Absolutely, but like a woman, not like a man looks. I believe that her search takes a course parallel to that of a man but in direct contrast to his, which puts them on a collision course to marriage.

He works; she works. He pays bills; she pays bills. Life deals him good and bad hands; life deals her good and bad hands. Education and opportunity are available to him; they are available to her. He loves the Lord; she loves the Lord. He is the hunter seeking the prize catch; she is the hunted and the prize. Parallel and contrasting.

I recognize that these terms hunted or prize, may not be attractive words, especially in this "I'm so sensitive" social environment, but I believe that they paint a spiritual visual that accurately identifies the players. My intent is not to give you some flowery presentation of the male-female relationship.

The issues of their lives are parallel, yet their responses and reactions to the same stimuli will in many cases be polar opposites. They are different beings, yet when they meet according to God's plan, they will somehow find the fit they could not find in all the other relationships. He will leave his father and mother and cleave to her (his wife) and in the sight of God they will become one flesh. Remember, the operative word is "become."

As we discuss the wife and her role, I want to reinforce the position of the woman and wife in terms of her equality and importance with men. We must remember that it is only the Word of God that is important in any discussion about what God has done. When we look back at Genesis 1:27, we can see again God's divine plan. He writes by inspiration of the Holy Spirit, "And God created man [mankind] in His own image, in the image of God he created him; male and female He created them" (NASB). In His divine creation, He created them in equality of being and established a hierarchy for continuity. God also says in his word in Genesis 1:28, "Then God blessed them, and God said to them, 'Be fruitful and multiply; fill the earth and subdue it, have dominion [rule] over...'" (KJV). Oh, what a wonderful word "*them*" is! I think it means both the man and the woman are to have equal dominion.

In this discussion about marriage, I want to be categorically clear that whether man or woman, we were created for one ultimate purpose and that is to glorify God. Therefore, the first thing that we understand about the man or the woman is as they travel on their paths to hunt and be hunted, they must have at the forefront of their minds and in the depths of their souls, not a wife, not a husband, but giving glory to God. Their lives should be submitted in obedience to God's Word, and they individually and collectively should be working in concert and cooperation with the Word by what they say and how they live their lives before others.

Now the woman who is to become a wife is to have her priorities in order. She must first love the Lord and then comes her husband. She learns this by applying herself to the service of the Lord while she is single, when her time is more available, as must the man also. She should attend herself to all that is available in ministry so as to strengthen her position in God. I can say without fear of reprisal or loss of esteem that my wife, Colette, loves the Lord more than she loves me. Trust me when I say that if there is one thing, I know about her, it is that God is first in her life and being. It is important to have that understanding.

You know I read somewhere, I don't remember where (perhaps it was Popular Mechanics), that, "wisdom is the chief thing, but in all thy getting get understanding" (Proverbs 4:7 KJV). You see, when God created man and woman, there was no level of authority except for God. The man and the woman walked in equality before Him. But after sin entered in, God established levels of authority on earth. Man and woman had dominion over the earth; they walked in equality before God and in concert and peace with each other. But we all know what happens when sin enters any situation: disorder, chaos, apathy, and anarchy. Because of sin, God had to institute a hierarchy of order. He chose to place man at the head, followed by the woman. As mentioned earlier, this order in no way pre-supposes the inferiority of the woman.

Just as a man must examine himself first to know who he is, so too must a woman. She must examine her experiences, her emotions, her background, and her relationships in order to take full stock of who she is because these are the things that she, like the man, will bring to the marriage. Self-control and the development of godly character along with integrity will make her a gift, a prize, and a good thing to her husband and likewise he to her.

Now, obviously there is much more to the issue of being a wife, and the intent here is not to try and provide an answer-all book. Instead the intent is to simply address some of the issues and keep at the forefront of the minds of men and women everywhere the seriousness of the institution of marriage and the divine importance of women in that institution. If women seek godliness, holiness, and righteousness as standards for their lives, then they will be the "good thing" that the scripture says a wife is to her husband.

CHAPTER 7

FAVOR

We now come to the issue of "favor," which is identified in the book of Proverbs as a benefit from the Lord that man obtains as a result of finding a wife. In the Hebrew tongue there are several words that are defined as "favor." The one that is related to this portion of scripture is the word "ratson" or "ratsown," which is linked to terms such as: acceptance, delight, good pleasure, good will, grace, kindness. By definition, this word is the concrete reaction of a superior to an inferior, particularly God. This word is used when God feels favorably disposed toward the petitioner.

According to Proverbs 18:22, when a man finally maneuvers his way through the maze of relationships which make up his life and finds himself cleaving to his own wife, God is then predisposed to be more accepting of the man, inclined to show him special good will and kindness that might not ordinarily be accessible to the man. It is my belief that when a man finds a wife, he is shown special favor because he has by choice entered into a divine covenant. We know from the study of the Bible God is resolutely sympathetic towards covenant. With God, covenant is the ultimate promissory note, which by God's holy standards should be dissolved only by death.

The Lord, in his infinite wisdom, does recognize that men, even men of old, had and have the liberty of availing themselves to the pleasures of womanhood without the binding cord of marriage. However, when a man chooses to join himself to a wife in holy matrimony for the purposes of God, he separates himself out from other men and allies himself with God, obtaining matrimonial favor through his wife who is the instrument of his release.

Now, Proverbs 31:10-31 identifies the wife's value, qualities, and influence, putting into perspective her unquestionable value to her husband, while at the same time and in the most palpable way revealing to us why when a man finds her, God would release favor to him. She is more valuable than jewels. Her husband can trust her. She nurtures. She is frugal and thrifty. Her strength and dignity come from her reverence for God. You will find that the psalmist does not mention the looks of the wife in Proverbs 31. She may be attractive, or she may not be, but her true attractiveness is bound up in her character. Arm candy is good until you need real nourishment.

Because she is this type of woman, it pleases God who in turn releases favor upon her husband. This may sound unfair to the unspiritual ear. It may sound as if she does all the work and he benefits from her efforts. But in truth, God is only being true to his order of authority and because she is who she is, God blesses her husband; and because her husband is a godly man, he recognizes her as the conduit of his blessings and is excited to share all that he has with her.

While studying one day, I came across a web page on my laptop entitled Anointed Word Ministries where they had an outline of "Ten Major Benefits the Favor of God Will Produce." As I reviewed those ten benefits, I was struck by how most (if not all of them) applied to my life and how they were directly correlative to my finding a wife. It was quite easy for me to draw a parallel between being married and those benefits of favor.

Here is a point at which a skeptic might interject and say, "Come on, Paul, if you look hard enough and close enough you can make almost any set of circumstances fit a particular situation"; and I would not disagree. All I am saying is that as I read over those ten benefits, my spirit was easily convinced that I had benefited from most of them since being married. It is not my intent to prove or disprove my statement or to challenge you to see if you can come to the same conclusion without having to stretch or distort your own reality.

The following is the list of benefits as outline in the web page article. See if there is any correlation between them and your relationship with your wife:

- Supernatural increase and promotion

- Restoration of everything the enemy has stolen

- Honor amid adversaries

- Increased assets - especially real estate

- Great and unusual victories, even in the midst of impossible odds

- Recognition and promotion, even when you seem to be the least likely one to receive it

- Prominence and preferential treatment, favor = kindness

- Petitions granted, even by ungodly civil authority

- Policies, rules, regulations, even laws (if necessary) changed (reversed) to your advantage

- Battles won in which you did not even have to fight, because God will fight them for you

Let me caution you that favor, of a Godly nature, is the result of relationship with and obedience to God and his Word. If your life is out of calibration, then the final results will be skewed.

As I look over the 33 plus years that Colette and I have been married, I can see clearly that many of these benefits were working in our lives. Some we were cognizant of at the time and some we were not. Some worked in combination with others, while some operated at individual stages; and still others are a part of prophesy for us. As I review these ten benefits and examine their effect on our lives, I am consciously aware of the reality that they were not perpetual but are discernible in their season of release.

After 33 years of marriage, I am still in awe of how the Lord has blessed me. If I had been left to my own devices, I am sure I would have ruined the lives of many father's daughters. Marriage for me is the pinnacle of success for my life. My wife and I both love the Lord, and we love being in His service. As a couple, we agree that we don't always have to agree with each other, but there is no denying that in order for us to make it, we must agree with the Word of God.

I know that some of you reading this might be inclined to say that I cannot be telling the truth, but I am. My wife is my best friend and I am hers. I can trust her because she fears God, and she can trust me, for the same reasons. We maintain mutual respect for each other and for the order that God has established. My wife is submissive to me but is in no way subservient to me. We have established a rapport of trust and confidence in each other that allows us to question one another without damaging the marriage.

Does my wife trust me to a fault? Ain't no way! (I know it's not proper grammar to use double negatives, but they emphasize my point.) My wife knows that I am a man and subject to human failings, and she is quick to remind me if the need arises. She does trust me enough to submit to me and honor me as is outlined in scripture. Does she call me "lord" like Sarah did Abraham? Don't even try it! But there is no doubt in my mind or heart that she does hold me in high esteem.

Husbands love your wife as Christ loved the church and gave his life for it. These are words of instruction from the Bible to husbands on how to promote a healthy and lasting marriage. Proverbs 5:15-20 speaks clearly to men and women about how important they are to each other and how they are to focus on their intimate relationship to the exclusion of all others. We find these words recorded from the Life Application Bible, New Living Translation: 15"Drink water from your own well – share your love only with your wife. 16Why spill the water of your springs in public, having sex with just anyone? 17You should reserve it for yourselves. Don't share it with strangers. 18Let your wife be a fountain of blessings for you. Rejoice in the wife of your youth. 19She is a loving doe, a graceful deer. Let her breasts satisfy you always. May you always be captivated by her love. 20Why be captivated, my son, with an immoral woman, or embrace the breasts of an adulterous woman."

We can see clearly from the scripture that the Lord's expectation for a husband and wife is that they remain faithful to each other and that their love remains exclusive. *"Drink water from your own well – share your love only with your wife."* How much clearer can the instruction to husbands and wives be? How is it that we have morally deteriorated so far that we are so easily tempted away from our responsibilities in marriage? As it was stated earlier, when we marry, there is really no clause that permits us to violate our marriage vows by seeking relationships outside of the marriage contract.

As I read scripture about marriage, I am more and more convinced that the majority of the responsibility for causing a marriage to be successful falls on the shoulders of the man. In this selection of Psalms 5, we can clearly see that the initial instruction is directed to the man. We can find example after example in the Bible of how every great man's fall into depravity is preceded by some immoral relationship with a woman not his wife.

It is, however, unfortunate for women that in many cases of infidelity or abuse, the men are more readily absolved of responsibility as culprits; and weight, shame, and blame for the indiscretion(s) becomes the scarlet letter worn by the woman.

CHAPTER 8

I AIN'T ASKIN

The previous points about women being viewed as the blame when men are found in infidelity or abuse is the perfect segue to say women, "DO NOT ALLOW YOURSELF TO BE A VICTIM!!" When Colette and I minister to men and women, especially in situations of infidelity and abuse, we always attempt to impress upon the abused their responsibility not to play the role of victim. You are in control. (I will explain from a more detailed and personal perspective in a moment.) We try to impress upon them [the abused] that the abused can never ask the abuser, "When are you going to stop abusing me?" The abused must make a conscious decision to refuse to be abused anymore. Don't ever be the victim; you have more control than you think. You are in control!

As promised, the following is my personal enlightenment. I am recounting this event as a means of instruction as well as a testament to my shame, but more importantly as a testimony to the courage of my wife. Heavy sigh! Ok, here we go.

When Colette and I had been married for only two months, we had just moved into our first apartment in North Hollywood, California, a brand-new building on Klump Street. One weekend, we were watching Colette's niece, Angel (I guess she must have been three years old, if memory serves me). The day was an ordinary day just like most others; however, the events of this day and the days, weeks and months, and years to follow would forever affect our relationship and influence my male consciousness.

The day had wound down and evening had turned into night. Colette was preparing a bath for her niece, and I was preparing for bed, mentally laying the groundwork for what I hoped would be a night of marital bliss with my new wife. I was anxious to be about my planned sexual exploits, and I felt like Colette was spending entirely too much time with this bathing activity and began to fuss about it. At some point Colette was running the hot water to warm the bath. Angel, her niece, reached up and touched the faucet, which had become hot, burning her fingers, and (as you would expect) began crying, loudly.

You may or may not have noticed that I keep referring to Angel as her [Colette's] niece, not our niece. Obviously, I'm making a point. I keep saying *her* niece because after only two months of marriage I had not established the type of familial bonds that would have allowed me to see Angel as my niece, too, allowing that her pain and discomfort would have been of the same concern to me as it was to Colette. What I saw was not a child in pain, but an impediment to my desired conjugal delight. Truth be told, it should not have mattered whether Angel was my niece or the child of a friend or neighbor. She was a person in need. What follows is the unfortunate results of the selfish mentality of the abuser.

Let me interject here, that I'm not implying that men only think this way and that nurturing is a gender specific characteristic. I am simply saying that abusers, whether male or female, are self-absorbed and for the most part insensitive to the needs and wants of others. As you would expect Colette, turned all her attention to Angel, attempting to calm her and attend to her burns; but in my narcissism, I became enraged because of the time it was taking to calm Angel down. Colette did all that she could to try calm me down and get me to understand that Angel needed her more than me. She was going to give Angel all the attention that she needed, and my desire for sex was the least of her concerns, which only incensed me all the more.

After a period of time, Colette got Angel calmed down, attended to her burns, and sent her off to sleep. This meant, in my mind, that I could possibly salvage a portion of my planned exploits. Tired and emotionally spent from dealing with an injured 3-year-old and an insensitive and brooding

31-year-old, Colette was not even close to wanting to be intimate. Yet I insisted, no, I demanded, that she perform her marital responsibilities. Colette made every effort to try and get me to understand that she was not physically, mentally, or emotionally in a place to minister to my needs and that perhaps another evening would work best for us.

That reasoning, although sound and mature, was nothing but an outright rebuffing and act of disrespect for my needs. How dare you! I am your husband and your provider and as such you should make yourself available to me and for me when requested, and your mental, emotional, and physical conditions are not my concern! I do not remember her response, probably blotted out by some weak attempt at rationalization. No, it's SHAME!! I do remember; however, my escalation and then more escalation and then...PHYSICAL ASSUALT! Not a push, a shove, a slap – but an all-out beating. Guess she'll really want to make intimate and passionate love after that.

Some perspective, at that time I stood five feet, ten inches and weighed around two hundred fifty pounds. Colette was five feet, three or four inches and weighed all of one hundred fifteen or sixteen pounds. Guess I showed her who the boss is.

After issuing what was a clear and concise message about who was in charge and how this marriage and household would run, I turned to walk out of the bedroom where I left my bride of two months battered and bruised on the bed, only to find myself weakened from severe pain in the top of my head and piercing pain on the cheeks of my face, neck and shoulders. Colette had sprung from the bed and attached herself like an octopus to my back, wrapping her legs around my waist, her right arm around my neck (she's left-handed), and with all the strength her soul could muster she began to pummel me about my head, face, and shoulders.

Needless to say, I was in shock and disoriented. The force of her blows disabled me. Somehow, I dislodged her (or she dislodged herself) and I stood face-to-face with this tiny, crazed woman who made it clear that if I wanted to engage in this physical relationship that she was more than up to the task.

As is true with all bullies and abusers when they are met with the same or greater force, their resolve to continue their behavior is greatly diminished. Also, like all abusers, when faced with the fallout of their indefensible conduct they feign contrition, and I was true to that truth.

I was sorry and remorseful and promised that it would never happen again, but that was a lie, or at least it would have been, if not for the actions taken by my wife, and not just her fighting back. I'll explain momentarily. It would have happened again because it had happened in the past, in my past, with other women – other girlfriends. I was no stranger to physical abuse in my former relationships and now, because I was married, was a professed Christian and an elder in the church, it was not going to change. I was not going to change unless the abused changed.

As I stated previously, I would have continued in my abusive behavior in my marriage if my wife had allowed me to. It was not just that she fought back. I grew up in a home were my mother and father fought like Ali and Frasier, and truth be told it was my mother who was the aggressor and instigator. They continued like that until I think they just got too old to fight. That pattern might have continued in my own marriage except for one significant action taken by my wife, Colette.

It was not her willingness to mix it up with me physically, but it was her determination not to be a victim by keeping it contained within the four walls of our home. After the beating, she called everyone she could think of: her mother, step-father, step-mother, natural father, brothers, the pastor of our church, deacons and board members, her friends and mine, locally and at a distance. If she had opportunity, I believe she would have taken out a full-page ad in the national papers.

She was not going to fall prey to shame and victim mentality by hiding the fact that her husband of two months was a wife beater. She was not going to take on the misguided mantle of reputation protector. "My husband is an abuser, and everyone needs to know! If he is concerned about his reputation, then he needs to take better care of it." This was her song.

I was out on "front street" as they say. There was no place for me to hide. There would be no made-up stories to explain the bruises; there would be no need for whisperings or conjecture about where they came from. They came from the hands and fists of the husband. "Yes, he beat me, and I want everyone to know." She made sure of it.

There was no hiding place for me. There was no sanctuary, not with friends, not with family, and especially not with my pastor who made me stand before the congregation and confess what I had done, like a man who pleads guilty in a court of law. Seeking favor, I had to make my statement of allocution before the congregation my behavior. For some couples, a time of counseling needs to happen, and I would recommend that route for most couples. However, for me the shame and public ridicule was enough counseling for me. To know that Colette not being afraid of me physically was significant, but more significant was the fact that she was not afraid to expose me. She would not ask me when I would stop abusing her, but she would just simply not allow it.

Colette and I have been married 33 years at the time of this writing and we have had our share of disagreements, but I have never put my hands on her since. We are best of friends, but there is one sadness that I carry beyond the shame of my abuse. I know that my wife loves me and that she knows I love her and would do anything for her, but I know that there is a place in her heart I no longer have access to and that is the place where she could say, "I know my husband loves me, and he would never hit me."

Again, if you are in an abusive relationship, married or single, don't hide the abuse; expose it. Don't protect a reputation, even yours; protect your life.

CHAPTER 9

GOD MALENESS COMPLEX

If men would be forthright regarding their infidelity, they would readily admit that they encouraged it to a large degree, or even pursued the betrayal. What man does not want to be seen as virile and attractive to the opposite sex? It's just sad that for many men proof of virility is associated with extramarital female conquest.

The unfortunate disadvantage to these conquests (other than the obvious hurt and distrust that is fostered) is that the women involved are more often than not seen as the culprits, and her feminine wiles are usually indicted as the instrument causing the indiscretion. The man, who has equal if not greater liability in the matter, is somehow viewed as a victim.

You may balk at my statement which, of course, is your prerogative; but the truth of the matter is that our society is more tolerant of the marriage indiscretions of its men than it ever would be for its women, dismissing them as some normal male rite of passage rather than the abhorrent disregard for the sanctity of marriage which it really is.

Just look at the issue of children out of wedlock. If a man makes a baby and decides not to own up to his responsibility, he's called a deadbeat dad; and if the woman is lucky, he might be forced to pay. Conversely, if that woman abandons her child, she is more likely to face public ridicule and possible legal repercussions. Now, you tell me that they are being held equally responsible.

I am not trying to "man bash," being a man myself; and I am definitely not excusing women from any culpability. I am concerned about making sure that men understand from a scriptural perspective that being the head of his household and the covering for his covenant relationship he is initially and ultimately responsible for protecting the sanctity and worth of his marriage.

He must ensure that he protects himself from temptation by first strengthening his relationship with the Lord and then applying as much energy and attention to his wife as possible. Attention does not necessarily translate into holding hands and taking long walks together daily but by providing her with an environment in which she feels secure and protected. Remember secure and protected for a man is not secure and protected for a woman.

Let me be cautious here because although men are called to head and protect their households, women likewise are called to help him to be as effective a head and protector as he can be. She cannot allow her frustrations or disappointments in him to cause her to stray from her responsibility.

He's not the same man that he was when you married him. Well, how could he be? His life experiences and responsibilities have changed. He is more and more aware of his frailty and mortality. The ravages of gravity and time have in most cases assaulted his self-esteem. He is battle weary and war torn and in need of respite.

I love my wife and I have matured to the point where more often than not my life and comfort are secondary to hers. It would be disingenuous to say that in every aspect of our relationship, even after 33 years, that I have conquered every issue. But I can say with all certainty that there are very few remaining. Do I love my wife, and would I give my life for her? For me, there is no doubt.

Now, if you want, you can have a conversation with my wife about her perspective on my previous statement of confidence. I pray that she would answer in the affirmative, but no matter, I believe that she knows that I do understand and take seriously my responsibility to love her as Christ loved the church and gave His life for it.

It is my disposition to believe that marriage is meant to be fun. We can get so hung up on would you die for me or do you love me more than life itself. Come on! How many of us are really equipped to even deal with that kind of question?

What about do you love me enough to respect me so as not to position me, or yourself, to have to ask such questions? Why don't we work on building our relationships and learning how to work through our challenges without destroying what we already have and then maybe, when we are 90 years old, we can sit and wax eloquent about the issues of love and life? Because by then she will not care if you will or will not die for her. She is probably wishing that you would hurry up and get on with it.

It is not important who is "right." What is important is that believers – especially married couples – work toward unity and agreement. A Godly and loving marriage is a partnership, in which two people are growing together as one (Gen 2:24; Matt 19:5, 6). A husband and wife must have many conversations and share their thoughts openly with each other in order to come to a place of "oneness" and agreement in their marriage.

My wife has a theory about what might be a major deterrent to men understanding women or their wives. I call it the "God Maleness Complex." What the heck is "The God Maleness Complex," you say? According to my wife's theory, men have trouble dealing with or accepting the significance of women and their roles because men believe either consciously or unconsciously that God is male and as such men vicariously are superior and women are of lesser import. I found it an interesting theory. Can you see how this idea could conceivably be the fulcrum on which we have tried to balance our male-female relationships, only to find that we are continuously out of balance with the scales falling disproportionately in favor of men because somewhere deep inside of our fragile male psyche we really do believe that God is male?

What we know from scripture is that God is "spirit" and is to be worshipped in spirit and truth. Since God is a spiritual being, He does not possess physical human characteristics. In scripture, figurative language is used to assign human characteristics to God in order to make it possible for man to understand God.

Let's not get caught up in the minutia of whether God is male or female, I simply wanted to give platform to what I believe is a viable theory from my wife as to why men and husbands may struggle in their relationships with their girlfriends and wives. And to be fair to this theory, there are plenty of women who believe that God is male. Just trying to balance the scales.

If we can kinda put a bow on this topic, the apostle Paul gives us insight into where this idea of male and female falls spiritually. Paul wrote in Galatians 3:28, "There is neither Jew nor Greek, there is neither slave nor free, there is no male and female, for you are all one in Christ Jesus." God loves us all perfectly. We are all one in Christ Jesus.

I love my wife not because she is my "help-meet/helpmate" and adds to me what is missing or needs supporting. I respect womanhood because it is ordained by God. There are three things in my life that I love more than anything else. I love my relationship with God. I love being married to my wife, Colette. I love being a father. All other things are suspect!!

No need to fear who we are, male or female, single or married; God has ordained purpose for each of us and his perfect love casts out fear. So, this brings me back to my initial question: *What's Love Got to Do with It?* The answer is simple, EVERYTHING!

ACKNOWLEDGMENTS

I want to acknowledge first, the most prolific, most insightful, and most relevant writer ever to put pen to paper. He is my inspiration for writing books and for living life. I acknowledge publicly that whatever I might write, no matter the length or how profound, it will pale in comparison to even one word written or spoken by this author - the Lord God Himself.

My words may bring some comfort, some correction and perhaps some hope, but His Word brings eternal life. To God be all the glory, now and forever.

I acknowledge my wife and best friend, Colette Joslin Toomer-Cruz. She has always encouraged me to exercise the giftings and talents given to me by the Lord and to trust Him no matter what and according to her, "It's no surprise to God!"

My children, Rachelle "Pip" Hunter, Geneva Colette Toomer-Cruz, and Gabriel James Engracia Benitez Cruz, each of you gives breath and worth to my life. I love you.

John "Dr." Hylton and Doris "Momma" Hylton as always, your encouragement and continued prayer is a private sanctuary and refuge for my heart.

To my church family, Love and Faith Christian Center, no pastor has ever shepherded a more loving, faithful, and benevolent ministry than you. You are giants in the Kingdom of our God. I am ever grateful to God for you.

To my friend NATION!! (that is me shouting) Zamar, your constant prodding and nudging was instrumental in getting my first book to print and the thought of having to put up with that again moved me to be more expeditious. Thank you, for caring that much.

Coach Rhyen Siemer, thank you for taking the time out of your summer to review and make the primary edits to my manuscript. You are a gifted basketball coach, from whom I have learned much under your tutelage, but your gift as the English Chair and instructor at Western Christian high school reaches far beyond the 94'X50'basketball court. Thank you, my friend.

To the administration and staff of Love Wins Publishing, thank you for the opportunity to see my second project come to fruition, but more importantly, thank you for providing a reasonably instructive platform for Christian authors, especially women and men of color.

CITATIONS

Of all the lines written for "*What's Love Got to Do with It*" album "You must understand though the touch of your hand makes my pulse react, it's only the thrill of boy meeting girl, opposites attract. It's physical, only logical, you must try to ignore that it means more than that …what's love got to do with it, what's love but a secondhand emotion…." (Britten, Lyle, 1984, Track 13)

10 Benefits of the Favor of God. (6 August 2019). Retrieved from https://anointedwordministries.org/

Available on Amazon

BOOK RECOMMENDATIONS

BY THE AUTHOR

Have you struggled with giving money to your church? Are you wondering if tithing is still relevant for the modern-day believer? Does God even care if you give or how much you give? If these questions have ever plagued your mind then KINGDOM DISTRIBU-TION, Cutting Covenant with God, will provide you with biblically-based principles to reassure you that your giving is not in vain and that through your giving your covenant with God is strengthened. Get your copy today on Amazon.com!

BY MRS. COLETTE TOOMER CRUZ

Pretty Sad is an anthology about the extraordinary strength of women. In Volumes I, II, and III of this powerful series, women from all walks of life have come together to expose every bruise, wound, and hurt from their past. In Volume IV, the mask and the makeup have been removed as the following women face themselves and their truth: Arisha Nabors, Colette Toomer Cruz, Fotima Hall, Freida Lorraine Queen, Jennifer Corona, Keci Monique, Latonya Littlejohn, Melissa McGill, Natasha Robinson, Nicole Miller, Shanea Farr, and Lead Author Tanya DeFreitas. Grab your tissue and follow along as these women tell the truth, the whole truth, and nothing but the truth! Available on Amazon.com!

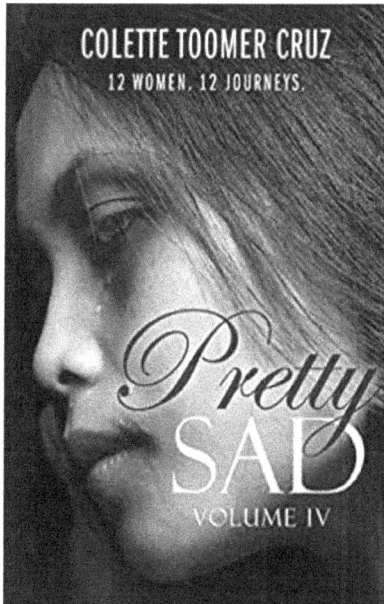